HOW TO GET
A JOB
IN THE WORST
OF TIMES

HOW TO GET A JOB IN THE WORST OF TIMES

Jay Michael Schechter

Copyright © 2012 by Jay Michael Schechter.

Library of Congress Control Number:		2012910183
ISBN:	Hardcover	978-1-4771-2522-9
	Softcover	978-1-4771-2521-2
	Ebook	978-1-4771-2523-6

All rights reserved. No part of this book may be reproduced or transmitted in any form or by any means, electronic or mechanical, including photocopying, recording, or by any information storage and retrieval system, without permission in writing from the copyright owner.

This book was printed in the United States of America.

To order additional copies of this book, contact:
Xlibris Corporation
1-888-795-4274
www.Xlibris.com
Orders@Xlibris.com
114519

CONTENTS

Acknowledgments 7
Preface..9

Long-Term Unemployed 11
Short-Term Unemployed..16
Currently Employed 20
Veterans 22
College Students..27
Note To Employers..32
Employment At Foreign Companies
    Both Domestically And Internationally 36

Appendix: List Of My Jobs Since College..42

ACKNOWLEDGMENTS

I wish to acknowledge the assistance and encouragement of Michael and Glenn Boutté. I am glad both of you guys put up with my long readings over the phone and became the cheerleaders for my persistence in finishing the chapters. You were there from the beginning encouraging me to write this book. I owe a great deal to both of you. A shout-out goes to Gerald Williams for also encouraging me to write this book and for emphasizing the need of this book for all those hard-core unemployed out there. You reminded me of all the experiences the both of us went through, and as I was writing this book, I kept those thoughts in mind. In addition, all the people who thought it was necessary for me to write this book in the first place: the people I must mention—Mark Boutté, the people at the Tacoma Social Security Office, and, finally, everyday people who I run into on the streets. You are the inspiration for this book. I also wish to thank Xlibris Publishing for editing and publishing this book.

PREFACE

There are three types of people in the world. Those that make things happen. Those that watch things happen; and finally, those that don't know what's happening.
—John Madden

We're not in a recession; your brain is in a recession.
—Glenn Boutte

An expert is a person who knows less about a subject longer than anyone else.
—Anonymous

This book is not a primer on how to get a job. There is no such book out. If there was such a book, it would be on the top of the best seller list, and everyone who has read it would find a job to their liking, and the United States would be close to full employment. I do not claim to be an expert on employment, nor will I give you a lot of facts and figures.

What I am saying is that those who take the initiative, don't dwell on events (whether they are good or bad), and don't listen to the so-called expertise of others are generally more successful in their employment pursuits.

If you want to confine yourself about other people's ideas on cracking the job market, go right ahead. I am not claiming to be the sole authority on obtaining a job. What I am claiming is that due to my own history of pursuing and obtaining jobs, I feel I can give you some pearls of wisdom. I am imparting my wisdom as a lifelong pursuer of jobs, having not been unemployed for any long period of time. In about forty years of being a veteran of the job market, I have worked eighty-five different jobs and counting. Granted some jobs were temporary and part-time; others were full-time, but not a good match, while others were career-oriented jobs. I worked for large companies as well as small ones, public as well as private concerns, and family-run and Fortune 500 firms too.

I shall give pointers to veterans, college students, the long- and short-term unemployed, as well as the currently employed.

I shall address employers and knock them down a peg or two. Then I shall explore working for foreign companies based here and abroad. In the final analysis, the prospective employee or current employee has to realize that no job is permanent and to remain adaptable or, as a friend of mine used to say, "mobile and agile."

Finally, I shall list all the jobs that I had since I graduated from college. The purpose of the listing is twofold: (1) to give you an idea of the length and depth of my job experience and (2) to prove that what I am saying is not science fiction.

LONG-TERM UNEMPLOYED

"There are no jobs out there."

"There are no more jobs out there in my line of work."

"Since the plant left town, no one has come in and replaced it."

"All the companies care about is themselves. They don't care about the people in this town."

"I'm too old to retrain for another job."

"Look at the number of the unemployed out there."

The above statements are some of the most common excuses for inaction. When something is not going your way, blame someone or something else. It is the most common rationalization for not placing responsibility on oneself and instead placing blame on someone or something else.

When one states there are no jobs out there, where aren't there any jobs out there, or when is someone out there not working? If there are no jobs out there, then no one would be working.

If someone states that there are no more jobs in his/her line of work, what they're saying is that what I have been doing for however long I have been doing it does not exist. So I cannot or will not adjust to the change by either adapting to the way the job has changed or transferring to another job that is suitable with my skills, aptitudes, or interests.

If a business leaves the area, does the town stop doing the daily activities of life? A town needs food, water, shelter, transportation, and raw materials for sales, manufacturing, marketing, and distribution to sustain the life of its citizens. A person needs a market to obtain food, the ground or field to grow food, the plant to build equipment for harvesting the food, a marketing network to distribute the food or the machinery. You need someone to sell the food or equipment for someone to buy these items. If there are people in your town, someone is performing these activities. Maybe these jobs are over in the next town or in the vicinity, or there would not be people there because they would not be able to survive.

A company's bottom line is to make a profit. A profit is the difference between staying or going out of business. A business is in a location because it needs a place to do business. This is what determines where a business is located and other factors. If the school system deteriorates, where that the type of person that comes out of it is not trainable, if the costs of water and sewage go up that the operating costs of the business become more expensive, or if there is no room for expansion—these and other factors determine whether a company stays in the area. A business does not have an open-end commitment to a town. Likewise, a person should have the skills, motivation, and flexibility to be employable not only for that particular business in town, but also to any business in any locality where the person and business would be a good fit.

REASONS FOR THE EXCUSES

Someone who is too old to retrain is saying that they're too old to learn another job, which means "I don't want to work any longer because every job you work at requires retraining or relearning new ways of working the old job or learning a new job to stay employable, or you will stay unemployed."

Let's take a look at the number of the unemployed out in the workforce. When there is an unemployment rate between 8 percent and 15 percent, there is at least 85 percent to 92 percent that are working. There are jobs out there for those 85 percent to 92 percent of the workforce, so someone must be hiring, or that many people would not be working.

To sum up what I said, in order to be employable, you need to be adaptable, mobile, and trainable. Let me also add one more attribute—that is, be communicative. In other words, you need to network. You need to go beyond your comfort zone, try something new, break down the barriers that you have been accustomed to since you were last employed. After all, if you are long-term unemployed, you have been unemployed for at least more than a year. By that criteria, if you made an attempt to find work, what you have attempted is not working.

STRATEGIES TO GETTING EMPLOYED

Using my techniques of adaptability, mobility, trainability, and communication, one can develop a strategy of getting employed, staying employed, and becoming employable in good times and bad.

Remember, the key to employability is finding a position that can get you employed and getting the hiring authority to hire you.

First, if you tried door-to-door knocking and resume writing to get the business to hire you, drop it. Very few, if any, employers hire someone off the street or by resume unless someone referred you to them and they requested a visit or a resume as standard procedure.

The key is to meet the hiring authority and get him or her to hire you. That is the only way to get employed.

Second, you have to *network* with people. Networking is a technique where you get to meet someone who knows someone who knows someone who knows someone who is hiring.

Third, you get recent experience, which means either getting a ground floor part-time job or doing volunteer work at a local charity or some type of community-based organization.

Fourth, look up jobs that you can either be trained in a short time or be quickly trained at a junior college or training center.

Last, when you find the type of job that's a fit or something you can perform, go global. What I mean is start local, within your city. Then go regional, state, national, and overseas.

How do you implement steps 2 through 4 that I just mentioned?

STEPS FOR IMPLEMENTING THE STRATEGIES

You have to start with yourself by asking yourself two basic questions: (1) How do I get a job or experience immediately to show other people what I can do? (2) What kind of work would be a good fit for me in case I want to stay in my existing job field, or should I switch into a different job field?

The answer to the first question is that there are two job categories that are always looking for people. One is volunteer work, and the other is telephone and/or customer service work. Volunteer work with a public or private agency helps you start the networking process of meeting people and generating contacts; and it gives you skills of customer service, phone handling and exposure to other types of skills such as data entry, inventory control, expediting, keyboarding on a computer, and a link to other skills if you prove competent to the person in charge. Volunteer work may not be paid work, but at least you develop two valuable assets: skills and contacts. Part-time phone sales jobs or other part-time paid customer service jobs also provide you with skills and contacts—only you get paid for the work you perform. If paid part-time work is not available in your area, try volunteer work. Either way, you will start to generate a job history that will look better to prospective employers than no job history at all.

While you are working part-time, you can spend your other time doing a self-assessment, which will answer the second question of working in your old job field or working in a new job field. A self-assessment consists of two parts: (1) what I am good at and (2) what the job market looks like now and down the road to see if my skills and interests match the jobs in the marketplace. The inventory can be done internally by yourself or by a job counselor or a vocational counselor at a community college, state employment center, or a nonprofit vocational service. The places I just mentioned can also provide you with the jobs most readily available now or in the future. You can also access job market information through the U.S. Department of Labor.

Next, once you find out the job that you seek, get your job skills upgraded or get retrained through a community college, a Joint-Training Partnership Agreement through the U.S. Department of Labor, a business, a union, a nonprofit agency, or a governmental agency.

While you're getting your training and working at your part-time job or volunteering, the final step is to network your skills and contacts locally and globally. I mentioned you are already networking in your part-time job or volunteering. You are also networking by associating yourself with instructors, union people, businesspeople, and college administrators while you are in training. You also need to join organizations that have local, state, regional, national, and international affiliates. Every field that has a business, union, nonprofit organization, or lobbying group is represented on a local, state, regional, national, and international basis. When you find these organizations, go out and try to join them. If it costs money, join as a volunteer or auxiliary member. These organizations have members that own businesses that employ people. Between the trainers, organizations, and the employers, circulating around these different groups will cause some prospective employer to possibly interview and hire you. After all, while you are working in, training for, and joining organizations, you are creating a wider network of contacts and thus potential employers who could contact you and eventually hire you once they are exposed to you. There is an old saying "No pain, no gain, no fame." If you don't apply what I am saying, chances are you won't have any fame, because no one out there will know you in order to hire you.

SHORT-TERM UNEMPLOYED

You have been laid off or have quit because you could no longer tolerate the conditions of your workplace. If you have been laid off, chances are that job you had will not come back because the company has moved, replaced you with a robot, or found it cheaper to replace you with someone else. If you have been terminated, because of either poor performance or because you were not a good fit for the company, you feel a sense of rejection or betrayal because of the amount of time and effort you put in for the company; and all you got for it was a pink slip and no income coming into your household. If you quit your job, you feel a sense of relief that you no longer have to go into the job dreading every minute. On the other hand, you worry when your next paycheck is going to come, and you have a steady stream of bills to worry about. You feel you can find yourself another job or perhaps go to work for yourself or with another partner.

Whatever the reason, you are unemployed for less than a year, do not have a source of income coming into your house, and are looking for work.

STRATEGIES FOR GETTING EMPLOYED

As a laid-off person, you have to face the reality that your job or your company is not there anymore. So you have to find a new company for your existing skills, upgrade your skills in your existing field, or retrain for a new line of work. Your first step, as I mentioned in the previous chapter, is to do a self-reassessment of what you want to do for a job and/or career. Again, assess your strengths and weaknesses either by yourself or through an employment counselor through a vocational battery. Next, find out what jobs exist either in your existing line of work or in another area, as well as what jobs are in demand now or will be in the future and would be of interest to you. As I mentioned in chapter 1, get in touch with the company where you used to work and get references from supervisors, cohorts, and other personnel who can vouch for your work there and who may know employers that are hiring. Next, find a group or association that company belongs to and either join the group or join as an associate if you don't have the money to be a regular member. The purpose is to generate contacts of employers. Remember, the key is to *network* so you can find your future employer. While you are generating contacts, you probably want to consider obtaining new skills in case your old skills no longer fit the job market.

First, consider a part-time job or volunteer work to either enhance new skills or get a steady stream of income while you obtain additional training. Remember, a part-time job or volunteer work is preferable to an employer rather than not working. In addition to your part-time job, retraining or enhanced training would be a good source of generating contacts and *networking* to meet people who may know contacts who may know employers. Follow up on your leads that you have developed through associations, training, and your part-time job and emphasize to them that you are willing to learn, work hard, and do whatever is necessary to make the firm thrive. It's a numbers game out there, and the greater the number of people you meet, the greater your chances are of being hired.

GETTING AROUND BEING FIRED

If you have been terminated recently—because of poor performance or because you were not the right fit for the company or some other reason—I wouldn't feel too bad about it. As a matter of fact, quite a number of people have been terminated from a job at one time or another. The key is to learn from that experience and move to another job. The first step is to get back into a job mentality. Just as I mentioned previously, you have to ask yourself, "What do I want to do with my career, and what steps do I need to take to get back into the job market?" Again, a self-reassessment of your goals and interests is in order: What types of jobs currently exist out in the market?

Do they match your abilities and interests? Once you have settled on a job or a career path, get yourself in a network mode through either a part-time job or volunteer work. Also, get references from the job where you were terminated or from previous jobs or personal references. So once you start networking from your part-time job or volunteer work and previous references, see if you need to upgrade your training through an apprentice program or junior college training if you want to stay in your current field. Or get more enhanced training at a junior college or a proprietary school if you want to make a career change.

GETTING BACK INTO THE GAME

Finally, once you're working and training, as well as developing your contacts and joining organizations, the law of averages will kick in; and you'll be collecting a paycheck once again.

Remember, don't focus on what got you fired—focus on what will get you hired! You can't dwell on something that has been done. Focus on your work life going forward. You'll probably look back on that job where you got canned and say to yourself, "Why did I stay at that cruddy job so long in the first place?"

The last group that I shall mention are those that just quit because they could no longer tolerate their job. There was a poll out recently that stated that the majority of working Americans say they were dissatisfied with their jobs and that of that majority, a considerable portion were thinking of quitting. The reasons given for quitting were numerous: not enough pay for the amount of work performed, cuts in pay and benefits, greater workloads, less time at home and more time at work, overdemanding management, and other reasons that were not given.

Some quit at the spur of the moment; others quit at a breaking point—when crossed, results in walking out the door. Others quit when a more attractive job is too good to pass up.

THINGS TO CONSIDER BEFORE QUITTING

Whatever the reason for quitting, there are certain things to consider before you quit. Unless you have something lined up, carefully consider the economic situation you would face when you do quit. Do I have enough money to tie me over between the time I leave my current job and the time I start my next job? Do I have enough job prospects waiting for me so I won't be financially strapped? Will the money that I already have in the bank for working cover the big immediate expenses such as mortgage, insurance, car notes, college expenses? Depending upon my age, education, and experience, will my future job offer me the same income as my previous job? Will my future job offer me the same level of income to maintain my standard of living? If you think about starting your own business or working for someone else, do you have sufficient income if either your own business or someone else's fails? The questions that I pose can determine how long you should stay at your current job or move on to your next job.

If you decide to move on to your next job, all the questions that I stated above, and in the previous chapter, come into play on your future job. You must continue to develop *networks* and ask the above questions in order to stay employable. The difference in your case is that it's your decision how long you want to stay at your current job or move on to greener pastures.

CURRENTLY EMPLOYED

We now come to the people that are left after the so-called Great Recession, and it's these people who are currently employed. However, as in chapter 2, of those who left their jobs because they could no longer tolerate their employer or wanted to take their career in a different direction or work for someone else, the majority of the currently employed are in the same boat as those who quit. The only difference is that the employed still work rather than quit.

There is an informal consensus in that lifetime employment is a thing of the past; and the informal agreement of you producing for the company and, in return, are rewarded does not exist anymore. In the present-day job market, you are left with two options: (1) work for the company long enough so you can qualify for a pension and/or benefits without being laid off or terminated or (2) read the tea leaves of where the company culture is going, and if you still have too much time left in order to qualify to even get a vested pension, develop a plan to ease your way out of your current company and either join another company or start your own business.

The one advantage you have over those who quit is that you're still getting income and have a chance to accumulate a nest egg in case you want to go to another job or develop your own job. Remember, unless you're close to retirement and the company is solid enough to pay out a pension and benefits for a lifetime, I would start developing my employment game plan as you're reading the print on this paper.

DEVELOPING THE EMPLOYMENT GAME PLAN

As I have been saying throughout this book, a company is in business to make a profit in order to stay in existence, not to keep you employed. What I just said about what a company is in business for is a fact of life in the business world. If an owner or CEO can keep their company going using automated equipment or moving somewhere else to produce a product more cheaply than employing someone, that will be the owner's or CEO's strategy. It is not a matter of loyalty or dedication to either the employee or the community; it's a matter of making a profit and staying in business.

What you have to do is develop a strategy that is in your best interest. You have to ask yourself, "What do I have to do job-wise and/or career-wise to develop a stream of income based on my financial interest by either working for someone else or working for myself and/or with a business partner?" After you answer the previous question, then you develop the same job-hunting strategies that I mentioned throughout the book. You need to affiliate with business customers, organizations, associations and other people who are club members, members of social organizations, associations, and fraternal groups to find a company that would be interested in hiring you at a job level high enough to maintain the living standards that you are accustomed to and a time frame where retirement is not a far-off prospect.

Again, you have to gauge the atmosphere of your company that just hired you to determine the length of your stay. If the dynamics of the company entices you where you think there is a mutual and cordial relationship for a long job tenure, stay; if not, start the job process as before.

I'll repeat this again: employment is based on a mutual relationship between you and your employer and/or partner that can be financially rewarding and beneficial to you as well as your employer or partner.

VETERANS

Veterans are as perplexing a group in attempting to find employment. Veterans are one group every segment of society is trying to assist in reentering the civilian workforce, yet they face one of the highest unemployment rates, particularly during periods of conflict and hard economic times. I feel there are two reasons for the unemployment phenomenon: (1) the misconception of the civilian population, particularly those of the agencies and groups that serve other populations who try to use the same methods and strategies in assisting the veteran, and (2) the misconception of the veteran as they try to reenter the civilian job market. The misconception of the civilian agencies is that there is a belief that all you have to do to assist a veteran is offer them a job or service or both, and the veteran will take advantage of the service and merrily assimilate into civilian life. For many veterans, there's a psychological and vocational readjustment most civilian agencies and services are not aware of. If a veteran served in a war zone, there is the traumatic stress of living on pins and needles of being on constant deployment and readiness, having to survive combat situations, and if injured dealing with the adjustments of impairments and disabilities as they come out of the conflict alive. Those veterans who work in noncombat roles have to deal with the constant stress of possible attack and monotony; even though they don't have to face the hazards of combat, they do have to face the regimentation of military life before work and after work and then back to their military quarters, where there is no breaking away from the military structure of constant rules, discipline, auxiliary duties, such as charge of quarters (CQ), police call, and constant monthly practice alerts in the middle of the night. In the military, you are on twenty-four-hour call, day and night, and you are made aware of it throughout your military life and on heightened alert in a war zone twenty-four hours a day.

WHY VOCATIONAL PEOPLE MISS THE MARK WITH MILITARY PEOPLE

Vocationally, the occupations and job classifications do not have similar titles with a civilian job in many classifications. A tank driver, infantryman, artillery gunner, and missile guidance operator have very few, if any, civilian job equivalents. With the vocational and psychological barriers that I mentioned, the expectation of the service person getting out of the military does not square with the position descriptions of the civilian jobs. Employers, job counselors, psychologists, personnel administrators, and service agencies have difficulty helping the veteran because of the semantic mismatch of what the military job title or specialty is and the civilian job title. What is needed by both the civilian and military sectors is understanding and communication of the transferability of skills from the military to the civilian world. Usually, the advice given by military and their civilian counterparts to the veteran is, "You have the GI Bill. Use it to go to college or get training somewhere." There isn't a realization by vocational counselors that you don't focus on job titles—you focus on transferability of skills. An infantryman uses a variety of tools in his pack (first aid kit, rifle with adjustable sites and automated attachments, compass, and shovel), and a tank driver uses a computer and laser-driven devices to put a fix on a target and an 88 mm turret with computer guidance systems to adjust coordinates to hone in on a target for a kill. Each of the military pieces of hardware that the soldier uses has civilian equivalent skills: body repair, surgical medical procedures, expediting, customer service, data entry, shipping and receiving, typing, and computer programming. Extrapolate the many military specialties to their civilian counterparts, and you have many civilian skills the employer can utilize.

As far as psychological challenges are concerned, the military is just beginning to get a handle on such issues as PTSD, shock, and the auxiliary impairments associated with these disabilities, which need to be treated on a comprehensive basis. However, I'm not going to deal with the psychological aspects of the veteran in this book. This subject has been dealt with by others who have much greater knowledge than me, and I claim not to be an authority on the psychological implications of military combat. The psychological aspect can be addressed in another book. Instead, I shall focus on the vocational readjustment of the veteran to the civilian world.

As I stated previously, the veteran has skills acquired in the military that can be transferred into the civilian job world. What needs to be focused on is taking these transferrable skills and having the veteran along with the vocational counselor and/or employer hone those skills for the veteran so it would be a good job fit for the veteran and the employer.

WHAT THE VETERAN MUST DO TO BE EMPLOYABLE

Although I got through mentioning the challenges that face veterans, the main responsibility for adjusting from the military to the civilian sector, as far as the job market is concerned, rests with the veteran. He or she must become the lightning rod of the transferability of job skills from the military to the civilian world, then take these civilian skills and network them through a variety of channels until the veteran becomes the right fit for the employer.

The job transferability phase can be done while the soldier is transitioning through an employment or job counselor on post or through a vocational counselor through the Veterans Administration. Once the soldier becomes familiar with their comparable civilian skills, then, as they become a veteran, they can use various contacts to network job contacts so they can become employable in the civilian workforce. One way of generating job contacts is through Veterans Service Organizations, or VSOs (American Legion, VFW, AMVETS, Disabled American Veterans, and others). These VSOs are organizations that consist of veterans who are either retired or work in the civilian sector and have contacts in the civilian workforce. The VSOs are the most veteran-friendly groups, and they are usually based at VA Hospitals or administrative centers, and they encourage you to join their organizations. Many of these VSOs have posts that are actual structures in which they hold meetings, perform various functions, and conduct social gatherings, which are a great way to network. Another group of organizations that are go-betweens with the military and civilian worlds are the various military associations (associations for the U.S. Army, Navy League, Air Force, and others). These associations locate and recruit at both military and civilian centers, where there are groups of active-duty military Reserves, military association members, and businesses that cater to the military such as contractors and VSOs. Another group that is quite receptive to the welfare of the veteran is the active-duty Reserves and National Guard units. Although a Guard and Reserve can be mobilized for active duty and were deployed for Iraq and Afghanistan, they drill usually one weekend a month, and drill with active duty units for two weeks out of the year. The Guard and Reserve consist of people who have civilian jobs, in school, or between jobs when they are not drilling; however, the Reserve center can be a meeting point for the VSOs and the military associations. Thus, the veteran has three points of networking for employers: Reserve/National Guard, VSOs, and the military associations. As far as becoming immediately employable, you can join the National Guard or Reserves while still on active duty within ninety days of separation from active duty. So while you are working part-time at least one weekend a month (more in some units), you can be developing job contacts, the three points of contact. Another organization that is an advocate of the veteran through the business community is the Employer Support of the Guard and Reserve, which consists of businessmen, government officials, and others who act on behalf of the Guard and Reserves in advocating that businesses give time off to their employees to drill and deploy on active duty. Not only are they advocates for the Guard and Reserves, but they are also the most receptive audience to veterans insofar as employment opportunities and are excellent points of contact with employers. When you advocate your job skills and work background, you at least have the Employer Support of the Guard and Reserve.

CHOOSE THE BEST OPTION FOR YOU

If you desire and need additional training to enhance your skills and/or develop your contacts, you can utilize the GI Bill for short-term and intermediate training (junior college or a proprietary school like

ITT, Everest, and so forth) or long-term training (four-year college or university and beyond). If you want both vocational options and additional training, you can pursue a temporary or permanent job through your contacts during the day and pursue your training at night through the GI Bill. Either way, you will be developing a continuous source of networks where you can develop your present career path and other career paths down the road. Whatever choice you make, the decision is yours.

COLLEGE STUDENTS

WHAT TYPE OF PATH DO YOU WANT TO PURSUE?

There have been misconceptions about college and the value of a college degree, particularly in the workplace. I'm not going to advocate either way about the benefits of college and the degree. What I shall say is that there are some things you should know about college and what you can contribute to your employment prospects. College is divided into two categories: (1) the four-year liberal arts college, which gives you a broad base liberal arts program in the arts and humanities, and (2) the public and private universities, which are either four-year programs (undergraduate or bachelor programs) or postgraduate programs (after you attained a bachelor's degree). The type of career path you want to pursue depends on the type of college you should attend. If your intention is to experiment with various areas of interest and come out with a piece of paper after four years, then the liberal arts college is probably your best bet. If you want to experiment your first two years and then settle on a field that you think will lead to job prospects, then the four-year university is for you. If you have already decided on a vocational track and want to specialize in a certain part of that vocational track, the university with both undergraduate and graduate programs would probably be your best bet.

WHAT YOU NEED TO WEIGH IN CONSIDERING HIGHER EDUCATION

You also need to weigh cost, the time you want to invest in your education, and the type of payback you want to get combined with your field of interest. When you weigh all the factors that I mention, you have to ask yourself, "Is at least four years of study worth the cost of an education and will at least lead to the type of career that I anticipate, or are there other alternatives that can lead to the type of career that I desire that is less expensive and less time-consuming? Those of you who have graduated or are about to graduate high school, thinking about reentering college, or are currently attending college constantly need to reassess the questions I pose and reevaluate the pros and cons of a four-year education.

Let me lay some tidbits of information from the Department of Labor. If current trends continue (and by all indications, they will), it is estimated that 70 percent of those jobs that are being created that are highly paid and require at least minimum technological skill do not require a college or bachelor's degree. The assumption that a four-year college degree will automatically lead to a high-paying job does not hold true anymore. Occupations such as school teaching that were once a gateway to the middle class are shrinking. The reasons for this are varied: Rejection of taxpayers of bond referendums to build schools, more accountability of teachers, cuts in education, higher pay, and less workload in other professions all result in less students entering the education field and even less graduates becoming teachers. Generally, those students who start out in the educational field change majors while in college. The result of all this is that there are more teachers coming out of college than there are teaching positions. The same trend holds true for other vocations besides teaching. Lawyers are now in such abundance that there are more lawyers coming out of law school than there are law firms that can hire them. I can go on and cite other examples, but the point is that the four-year degree plus graduate degree doesn't necessarily lead to a job at the end of four years.

This is not to say that college is a useless endeavor and that you should save money going to a junior college, proprietary school, or other training program. What you need to do before you fill out the college applications is research the field that you want to pursue and see what type of job prospects await you at the end of four years. There are fields like software development, where you're literally guaranteed a job in which you need a degree in computer science or IT as a prerequisite or in health care administration or other fields that will be in great demand now and in the foreseeable future. Remember, it is not any degree that is essential, but the type of degree that you pursue that determines your employment prospects.

STEPS YOU NEED TO PURSUE IN COLLEGE IN LIEU OF THE JOB MARKET

Let's assume you want to pursue a field of study, after researching job prospects in that field, that appears to be in demand; and you select the university you wish to attend. Since the four-year liberal arts college is out because it focuses on very general areas of study and is not intended for vocational areas of interest, you then need to focus on your next priority in college in preparation to make yourself employable. Preparing yourself for the job world in college is no different from pursuing a job outside of college, and that is *networking* (sounds familiar, doesn't it?). Once you're on track with your academic studies, you should then seek out activities and interests that would help put you in contact with sources that can help get you into that track for a job or career. One of the sources is a club or professional business fraternity, which has both men and women members. Even though they call it a fraternity, it is more of an association that can put you in touch with professional contacts in the college campus and at the job site. Another source of *networking* is *internships*. An internship is where a business in your field of interest hires prospective employees such as college students, sometimes paying a *stipend*, which is a small salary, in order to determine if the prospective employee would possibly be a good fit for the firm and provide actual work experience outside of the classroom to see if this is the field that the student wants to pursue for a career. In mentioning the *internship*, it can be a semester or a year, full-time or part-time; and the duration can be a day, week, month, semester, or year, sometimes two years depending on the company. You can find out about internships through the department, business fraternity, or association.

KEYS TO SUCCESS IN THE JOB WORLD

There are two attributes one needs to be successful in the job world: (1) competency and training, which you can gain through the classroom, departmental club/fraternity, and internship, and (2) interpersonal relationships, which one might attain mixing and associating with a diverse group of people. One can get this experience in college by joining a social fraternity or sorority. In a fraternity or sorority, one can mingle with different people (not all people in a fraternity or sorority look alike or think alike), which can help you connect with a network of contemporary and older brothers or sisters who can connect you with a family-like structure working in all areas of the business world. These contemporary and older brothers and sisters can extend your network as far as employers and resources and perhaps become a link to your first job in the business world and subsequent jobs down the line.

OTHER RESOURCES TO HELP YOU IN THE JOB WORLD

Once you graduate, you can avail yourself of the *alumni association* for as long as you live. The *alumni association* is a group of college graduates who affiliate with the college to bring former college grads together for different activities and put out a newsletter and other activities. One important activity that the association handles is a job resource center, which you can access anytime while in college or after college. So if you are thinking about changing jobs or careers, the center would be a good place to start. The alumni association avails itself to you usually during your senior year and orients you to their services.

IT'S UP TO YOU WHAT RESOURCES YOU WANT TO UTILIZE

The choice is up to you what activities you want to pursue while in college. Some people are turned off by the Greek social system and would rather pursue the academic clubs, fraternities, and associations, which is fine. However, the important point is don't just depend on your grade point average (GPA) to get you into the employer's front door. You need to combine the academic with the experience (internships), contacts (academic clubs, fraternities, or associations), and, as an additional option, social fraternities and sororities. These are your gateways into the networks and contacts to connect to your prospective employer, so take advantage of them. In good times or bad, it is a competitive world out there, and you need every resource at your disposal.

NOTE TO EMPLOYERS

"The difference between the way I operate and American companies is that I put my employees first, the customer second, and the stockholder last, whereas American companies put the stockholder first, the customer second, and the employees last. If you treat your employees well, they will treat the customer well, which in turn will reflect in the bottom line for the stockholder." The statement that I just quoted from was from Richard Branson, founder and head of Virgin Inc., one of the largest international conglomerates in the world. Virgin has a reputation for treating their employees well and attracting top-flight employees, which makes the Virgin name synonymous with quality and translates into billions of dollars in sales throughout the world. Virgin produces these results by giving each of their companies and employees the latitude to be creative and innovative in bending over backward for the customer in which some of the aspects of their service would seem outrageous not only to their competitors but to other businesses in general. In return, employees are rewarded well for their efforts with money and recognition. On the other hand, most businesses have not achieved the astonishing growth that Virgin has achieved since Branson founded the company in 1970. As far as stockholders are concerned, one of its companies, Virgin Media, just became a publicly traded company on the London Stock Exchange, which shows that you don't have to be a large publicly traded company to get the type of results that Virgin achieves.

I'm not trying to encourage you to go on the London Exchange and buy Virgin Media. I'm trying to illustrate the point that employee satisfaction results in customer satisfaction, which eventually results in growth and productivity for the company, and for the stockholder, if publicly traded, in increased shareholder value.

HOW A COMPANY TREATS ITS EMPLOYEES IS CRITICAL IN THE GLOBAL ECONOMY

The point I'm trying to make is in today's economy, operating in a global climate with abrupt cyclical changes, any movement in market, product, quality, and customer service can determine the outcome for any business, public or private. How a business treats their employees can affect the market, the quality of the production of the product, as well as distribution, and the type of customer service that the customer receives.

Over half of employees today working for American companies are so unhappy with their employers that the thought of quitting has crossed their minds if only there were job prospects awaiting them. If all the companies in this country treat their employees the way Virgin Inc. treats their employees, I would not be writing this book.

WHY I AM WRITING THIS BOOK

The reason I am writing this book is to warn employees now and in the future not to be in for a surprise when a relationship between employer and employee breaks down, resulting in low productivity, high absenteeism, and general apathy in the workplace, resulting in poor customer service, substandard quality, and a drop-off in sales and customer satisfaction—spelling trouble for the company. This is not rocket science. In such a climate, the employee must develop a proactive strategy of looking elsewhere in using networking and generating outside relationships in order to stay one step ahead of their employer to avoid adverse job actions, such as a layoff or termination. Public schools and business administration programs at universities have been stating the problem of managing employees time and again, and that is how a company manages people. Business consultants from Frederick Deming to Tom Peters state in books and on the lecture circuit that good companies have effective management skills and involve their employees in the business process from planning to production to distribution. Seminars state this to employers till it sounds like a broken record. You don't have to take my word for it. Check out your own shop and either participate in an informal group discussion or schedule confidential one-to-one interviews and let your employees speak their mind. What you'll get will probably surprise you if you lock yourself in the office. The responses will probably range from "The boss doesn't want to hear my suggestions or downplays them" or "Why can't we get some more help or even temporaries to help out with the workload?" "These long hours and all this mandatory overtime is affecting my home life, with less time to spend with my wife and kids." "I work so many days and hours during the week and on weekends that I am ready to drop and don't have any energy left." "Why am I contributing more to my benefits package, and they freeze my pay?" "Why do they freeze promotions, and don't they reward us for doing a good job?" "They want us to produce more with less people and resources." "When we get an e-mail telling us about a new product line or procedure, no one explains to us the details or gives us instructions either in a group meeting or in a training session."

THE PROBLEM IS YOU

If your reaction is "Well, if they gripe so much and are unhappy with the way things operate here, they can go elsewhere" or "The door swings both ways," the problem is not with your employees—it's with you. You're not hearing what they're saying. The reason they are griping and making suggestions is they care about the conditions that go on in the workplace and how it affects their productivity, which affects quality and, ultimately, customer service and eventually profits, which is the lifeblood of the business. The employees do care about the business, or they would not be complaining. After all, they spend most of their waking hours in your place of business, so what they do during the workday ultimately affects their lives outside the workplace. If they feel that management appreciates them, it translates into a more productive relationship between you and them, which in turn translates into a more effective workday in the workplace, which in turn results in greater job satisfaction and even higher productivity. If the door swings out and the employees take a hike and go elsewhere, chances are they will either go to your competitors or some other employer, with high skills and ready to start anew with a new employer. The end result with you is that you lose workers with skills that are difficult to replace, and it will cost you more to replace and train new employees. In addition, word of mouth from your former employees gets around, and any new employees will just as likely take a hike as your previous employees. This cycle will result in greater costs to you, which will take away from the time and money you could put in a plant and equipment as well as training, which would further decrease the profits of your business.

Mr. Employer, if there is anything you should extract from this chapter, it is the need to listen to your employees. Take heed of what they are saying, involve them in all phases of the business from initial decisions to the final product, reward them if they meet or exceed expectations, and finally complement them when they do a good job. If not, you'll find your business listed in the classified section under the caption "Out of Business."

EMPLOYMENT AT FOREIGN COMPANIES BOTH DOMESTICALLY AND INTERNATIONALLY

As I quoted Richard Branson at the beginning of the last chapter, I forgot to mention he is a British citizen and that Virgin is a foreign company. However, you probably guessed that he is from outside the United States when he compared himself to American corporations. This leads me into asking, Why should you be in the mind frame of working for an American company and risk losing your job, when you could be working for a foreign-based company?

BRIEF HISTORY OF MOBILITY TO THE UNITED STATES

This country was composed of foreign-born people who migrated from all corners of the globe to find better opportunities here. Vice versa, if better opportunities exist with a foreign company that has subsidiaries here or overseas, why not take advantage of the opportunity if your relocation and work permits are covered by that company? As I stated before, it is now a global economy where both people and companies move; and whether you like it or not, it will remain that way for quite some time.

AMERICAN OUTSOURCING

Let me shed some light on American companies. The fact that these companies have been Purchasing American parts and equipment, and hiring American workers is a myth. Since at least the 1970s, when Chrysler nearly got a bailout from the government, there was a discovery that nearly half the parts that go into Chrysler cars came from overseas manufacturers and distributors. Recent reports about American companies outsourcing plants, parts, and equipment and contracting out people overseas is not a new phenomenon. Again, the process started in the 1970s when American companies started en masse to build plants and hire workers overseas. The surge of Japan in the 1980s with the publishing of books such as *Japan as Number 1 a*nd *The Reckoning* by David Halberstam highlighted the decline of American manufacturing and the relinquishing of American superiority in autos, electronics, video equipment, and other products to the Japanese. Part of the Japanese surge was the result of American expertise, plant, and personnel outsourcing to Japan. In the 1990s, American companies made record profits, but a large result was the growth of their foreign subsidiaries compensating for the relatively flat growth back home. The NAFTA Agreement resulted in accelerating outflow of U.S. companies and jobs, which was later acknowledged by proponents of the agreement such as Bill Clinton. It was once said that "what is good for GM is good for the country." The phrase should be reworded to "What is good for GM is good for Japan, China, or any other country you want to insert in that phrase."

Well, that phrase holds true for employees as well as companies. If Chrysler or GM can go overseas to seek greater horizons, so can the American worker. There is no law that states you can't work for a foreign-based company in the United States or overseas. As a matter of fact, there are thousands of American workers that are employees of foreign-based companies in the United States and overseas. I shall go even further and state that every major foreign corporation has an American subsidiary.

KEYS TO EMPLOYMENT WITH A FOREIGN-BASED COMPANY

Now that I have established the fact of a foreign presence in American business, let me elaborate on how the American worker fits into this mosaic. It has been the case of American business folklore that businesses seek qualified workers to fill positions that require greater skills than before in order to handle the increasing technological equipment and processes that American businesses are incorporating into their workplace. It is also stated and reiterated by American businesses and their proponents that American corporations have to go overseas to find skilled workers to fill these positions because of the lack of skilled workers back home. If the previous sentence is true, then why are leaders of foreign businesses quoted in saying that they are increasingly requesting American workers to man generalized positions in China, Japan, Europe, as well as in the United States? It has been stated by heads of foreign corporations that American workers can adapt to constantly changing conditions more quickly than their foreign counterparts and are more innovative and creative in the problem-solving and decision-making processes.

PROBLEM WITH AMERICAN MANAGEMENT

If the above statement holds true, then why is the American corporation not hiring more American workers? Cost could be part of the answer, but cost does not explain the constant shift of American plants to other countries or even back to the United States. I think the answer lies with American management. The former head of Sony Corporation Akio Morita stated back in the 1980s, and seems to hold true today, to an American reporter, "The day that I fear American corporations is the day that they know how to manage people." He made the statement because a Sony plant near San Diego outperformed the Sony plants in Japan. The same results hold true when American subsidiaries are in competition with their foreign contemporaries in other industries. Year after year, industry after industry, Americans outproduced and outperformed their foreign cohorts with the same degree of quality and excellence in their work.

STRATEGIES TO GET EMPLOYED WITH A FOREIGN-BASED CORPORATION

So what is the American worker to do when the above dynamic continues to hold true? The answer seems to be to stop doing the same thing and try something different, and that is to develop strategies of networking and making contacts to seek employment with foreign companies both here and abroad. For example, the chief interface for the conglomerate of Japanese companies, or *keiretsu*, is the Japanese equivalent of the U.S. Chamber of Commerce and the U.S. Trade Mission; and that organization is called MITI, whose function is to coordinate and promote trade and also advocate and direct growth in certain industries and work in conjunction with these industries to spur economic growth and job development. So if one knows people in MITI, they can perhaps gain insight into finding out how the players are cultivating relationships, because with Japanese companies, relationships are a critical part of doing business. How does one establish a relationship? This is done by joining various associations and groups that promote Japanese-American business relationships on a formal or informal basis. Such associations would be the Pacific Rim Group, the Japanese Chamber of Commerce, the U.S.-Japanese Trade Partnership, and other groups. Also, American subsidiaries of foreign companies have personnel departments where you can apply; but just as in American companies, you have to know the people who are doing the hiring because that is how you get employed. Each foreign company, other than Japanese companies who have subsidiaries in the United States, has a different culture and protocol; but the groups and associations they affiliate with are the same in nature. So it's good to familiarize yourself with these groups and begin to generate contacts.

Since one is dealing with a foreign company whose traditions and culture are different from that of an American company and, as an American employee is not certain how to get your foot in the front door, where do you start? Again, as with an American company, the answer lies in networking. Get to know and acquaint yourself with the links that have access to those foreign corporations; and foreign missions, embassies, foreign chambers of commerce, foreign institutes, and universities that have foreign studies departments are the keys to those links. Just as the foreign company establishes links with the institutions that I mentioned above to acquaint, know, and work with those parties that help set themselves up in the United States, so it is with the foreign institutions to acquaint, know, and collaborate with to get employed with a foreign corporation.

Another method of generating contacts in order to get hired by a foreign corporation is finding out the Americans that work for these companies and having them become the link to their supervisor or some other person who does the hiring to get you into that interview and the job. The same holds true for a foreign corporation as well as an American one; tell them what they want to hear and pitch it to them. Most managers want to hear two things: (1) that you're flexible and are willing to multitask and (2) that you're a team player and are willing to work long hours to achieve the desired results.

I just mentioned working for an American subsidiary of a foreign corporation. Perhaps you feel there are a limited number of opportunities in the United States with a foreign company and you want to land in the country where the corporation is based, how do you go about the process of working where the company is home based? The answer is it's kind of difficult unless you have citizenship in that country or have lived there and know the people and customs. As I stated before, each country is different; however, most countries require a work permit or work visa, which requires that you establish or intend to establish residency in that country. You can establish residency if the company that hires you would be willing to sponsor your residency based on a work permit or visa and eventually get residency if you work in the country long enough. However, most businesses shy away from sponsoring a foreign worker because of the pressures of hiring a domestic worker over a foreign worker unless the job is a critical skill in which the company cannot find a domestic worker that possesses those skills. Your best bet is to stay at the U.S. subsidiary for a while, travel to the country where you would like to work and is home based to the country, and get to know the people over there who work for the company.

MAYBE A FOREIGN COMPANY IS RIGHT FOR YOU

In summation, the employee has options other than staying with an American corporation or waiting for an American company to hire them. The foreign company gives the American employee leverage to jump ship from an American company if it is not right, and a new career path awaits them with perhaps greater career opportunities and better working conditions. The fact that not more American workers are checking out foreign-based corporations in the United States remains a mystery. However, if American corporations do not pay attention to the American worker, as I mentioned in the previous chapter, American employees will go to a company with a foreign flag sailing above its plant; and U.S. companies will be waving the white flag as they relinquish their economic dominance to foreign-based plants.

APPENDIX: LIST OF MY JOBS SINCE COLLEGE

Now that I have written a how-to book on job-hunting and networking techniques, let me elaborate on why I wrote this book and why I am listing my jobs since I graduated from college. I couldn't silently sit by while reading about jobs going begging, reading and hearing stories about the increase in the number of new jobs across the county while, at the same time, reading stories about the unemployed complaining that there are "no jobs" out there in the job market. On the other hand, I was changing jobs like there was no tomorrow with little difficulty. I then asked myself, "Why was it so easy for me to find work and change jobs, even when I sat out recently for ten months, on my own choosing, then got back in the job scene with not one offer but several offers of employment?" On the other hand, I read and hear about chronically unemployed people out there with skills ranging from unskilled to highly skilled who can't find work. I discovered that the answer isn't the lack of jobs in the market, but the way one goes about seeking work, which is the crux of the issue. As I stated before, I have and continue to work jobs ranging from short-term temporary to full-time permanent, with a full benefits package. As a matter of fact, I just retired from my last job with a pension and lifetime health insurance.

I'm going to list these jobs, but I am not going to give the name of the firm because the company name isn't important; however, I will designate the type of company or the function of the company. The reason I am listing these jobs is because the number of jobs that I have worked have surpassed most people's employment history by a generation or two. It has been stated by other people when I briefly list the number of jobs that I had that I could write the Dictionary of Occupational Titles (DOT), which is used by employment and rehabilitation counselors, as well as people in the personnel field to analyze jobs, assign skill levels and characteristics, and match a person up with a job. I shall now list the jobs I had since college, so here we go:

TITLE	LENTH OF TIME	REMARKS
Furniture Mover	Jun-Sep '70	Military Base
Teacher	Sep-Oct '70	Public School
Soldier	Oct '70-May '72	Military
Teacher	Sep '72-Mar '73	Public School
Teacher	Mar-Apr '73	Private School
Job Placer	Apr-Oct '73	Private Agency
Shipping Clerk	Oct '73-Mar '74	Tool Distribution
Assistant Manager	Mar-Aug '74	Paint Store
Keypunch	Aug '74	Car Parts
Supply Clerk	Jul '74-Jan '75	Reserves
Inventory Clerk/ Assistant Foreman	Aug '74-Jan '75	Sign Company

Clerk-Typist	Feb-Dec '75	Work Study
Medic	Feb '75-Jun '76	Reserves
Door-to-Door Canvasser	Jan-Aug '76	Remodeling
Records Clerk	Aug '76-Jun '78	Hospital
Canvasser	Jun '78	Frozen Foods Meat Sales
Records Clerk	Jul '78	Welfare Department
Data Clerk	Aug-Oct '78	Federal Agency
Telemarketer	Oct '78	Home Improvement
Telemarketer	Oct '78	Home Improvement
Telemarketer	Nov '78	Home Improvement
Legal Clerk	Dec '78	Reserves
Partner/Owner	Oct '78-Jan '79	Home Improvement
Medical Billing	Jan-Apr '79	Medical Insurance
Benefits Clerk	Apr-Sep '79	Phone Company
Security Clerk	Sep '79-Feb '80	Phone Company

Benefits Clerk	Feb '80-Jan '81	Phone Company
Linguist Clerk	Jun '81-Apr '82	Reserves
Administrative Clerk	Jan '81-Aug '82	Phone Company
Administrative Clerk	Apr-Aug '82	Reserves
Telemarketer	Aug-Oct '82	Home Insulation
Telemarketer	Oct-Nov '82	Magazine Subscriptions
Telemarketer/ Crew Chief	Oct '82-Jan '83	Home Insulation
Sales Rep	Jan '83	Billboard Company
Sales Rep	Jan-Feb '83	Copy Company
Telemarketer	Feb-Apr '83	Home Insulation
PBX Operator	Apr-Dec '83	Phone Company
Data Clerk	Jan-Oct '84	Phone Company
Clerk	Jun '83-Jan '85	Reserves
Air Cargo Specialist	Jan '85-Mar '86	Reserves
Network Operations Clerk	Oct '84-Aug '86	Phone Company

800 Data Clerk	Aug '86-Sep '87	Phone Company
Car Salesman	Sep-Oct '87	Car Dealer
Telemarketer	Oct '87-Jan '88	Magazines
Telemarketer	Oct '87-Apr '88	Insurance
Tariff Clerk	Apr-Sep '88	Phone Company
Telemarketer	Sep-Oct '88	Computer Company
Records Clerk	Nov-Dec '88	Defense
Contract Clerk	Dec '88-Apr '89	Defense
Telemarketer	Jun-Aug '89	Magazines
Quality Assurance Clerk	Apr-Nov '89	Defense
Airline Agent	Nov '89-Jun '90	Airline
Telemarketer	Jul '90-Jan '91	Computer Company
Computer Operator	Jan-Feb '91	State Agency
Legal Processing Clerk	Feb '91-Jul '92	Government
Legal Processing Clerk	Jul '92-Mar '93	Government

Records Clerk	Mar-Jun '93	Government
Independent Contractor	Jun-Aug '93	Nutrition Company
Telemarketer	Aug-Dec '93	Home Improvement
Telemarketer	Jan-Feb '94	Billboard Ads
Telemarketer	Feb-Jun '94	Office Products
Clerk	Jun '94-Jun '96	State Agency
Salesman	Jun-Aug '96	Office Equipment
Interviewer	Sep '96-Feb '97	Research Center
Administrative Assistant	Mar-Aug '97	Office Equipment
Telemarketer	Sep-Dec '97	Insurance Agency
Interviewer	Jan-Mar '98	Research
Telemarketer	Apr-Jun '98	Insurance Agency
Customer Service Rep	Jun-Aug '98	Retail Credit Card Center
Fiscal Secretary	Aug '98-Mar '99	State Agency
Telemarketer	Mar-Apr '99	Insurance Agency

Legal Clerk	Apr '99-Jul '00	Government
Contact Representative	Jul-Oct '00	Government
Sales Representative	Oct '00-Jan '01	Phone Company
Laborer	Jan-Apr '01	Temporary Labor Agency
Interviewer	Apr '01-Mar '03	Research Company
Interviewer	Apr-Sep '03	Research Company
Legal Assistant	Sep '03-Sep '07	Government
Legal Assistant	Oct '07-May '09	Government
Case Manager	Jun-Sep '09	Government
Census Taker	Apr '10	Government
Secretary	Jun-Jul '10	Government
Legal Assistant	Aug-Sep '10	Government
Legal Assistant	Jul '11-Feb '12	Government (Retired)

Since I started this book, I have retired from the government with a full pension and health insurance.

I am counting the same title more than once because they were at a different location from the previous location and may have involved different duties. As I stated before, I worked full-time and part-time for both large and small firms. I worked the range from laborer to management. By the way, if you're curious, I had a total of eighty-five jobs since college; and since I retired, it looks like I shall be starting number 86 shortly. May your job hunting be as fruitful as mine.

www.ingramcontent.com/pod-product-compliance
Lightning Source LLC
Chambersburg PA
CBHW021048180526
45163CB00005B/2331